THE BEATLES

RECITAL SUITES FOR PIANOFORTE

ARRANGED BY PHILLIP KEVEREN

— PIANO LEVEL —
LATE INTERMEDIATE/EARLY ADVANCED

ISBN 978-1-5400-2658-3

Visit Hal Leonard Online at
www.halleonard.com

Visit Phillip at
www.phillipkeveren.com

Contact Us:
Hal Leonard
7777 West Bluemound Road
Milwaukee, WI 53213
Email: info@halleonard.com

In Europe contact:
Hal Leonard Europe Limited
Distribution Centre, Newmarket Road
Bury St Edmunds, Suffolk, IP33 3YB
Email: info@halleonardeurope.com

In Australia contact:
Hal Leonard Australia Pty. Ltd.
4 Lentara Court
Cheltenham, Victoria, 3192 Australia
Email: info@halleonard.com.au

PREFACE

These suites were written to be concert showpieces for advanced students or professionals. They were designed both to honor the integrity of the original songs and to provide the accomplished pianist with serious material worth rehearsing and presenting.

Four albums are featured: *A Hard Day's Night* (1964), *Meet the Beatles* (1964), *Help!* (1965), and *Rubber Soul* (1965).

I was a Beatles fan long before writing these suites. In the process of seeking out the instrumental possibilities for the pianist within the tapestry of the original recordings, my admiration for the songs themselves only deepened.

Phillip Keveren

BIOGRAPHY

Phillip Keveren, a multi-talented keyboard artist and composer, has composed original works in a variety of genres from piano solo to symphonic orchestra. Mr. Keveren gives frequent concerts and workshops for teachers and their students in the United States, Canada, Europe, and Asia. Mr. Keveren holds a B.M. in composition from California State University Northridge and a M.M. in composition from the University of Southern California.

CONTENTS

4 **A HARD DAY'S NIGHT**
AND I LOVE HER
CAN'T BUY ME LOVE
A HARD DAY'S NIGHT
I'LL BE BACK

20 **HELP!**
HELP!
IT'S ONLY LOVE
TICKET TO RIDE
YESTERDAY

34 **MEET THE BEATLES**
ALL MY LOVING
I SAW HER STANDING THERE
I WANT TO HOLD YOUR HAND
IT WON'T BE LONG

50 **RUBBER SOUL**
DRIVE MY CAR
IN MY LIFE
MICHELLE
NORWEGIAN WOOD (This Bird Has Flown)

A HARD DAY'S NIGHT

Words and Music by JOHN LENNON
and PAUL McCARTNEY
Arranged by Phillip Keveren

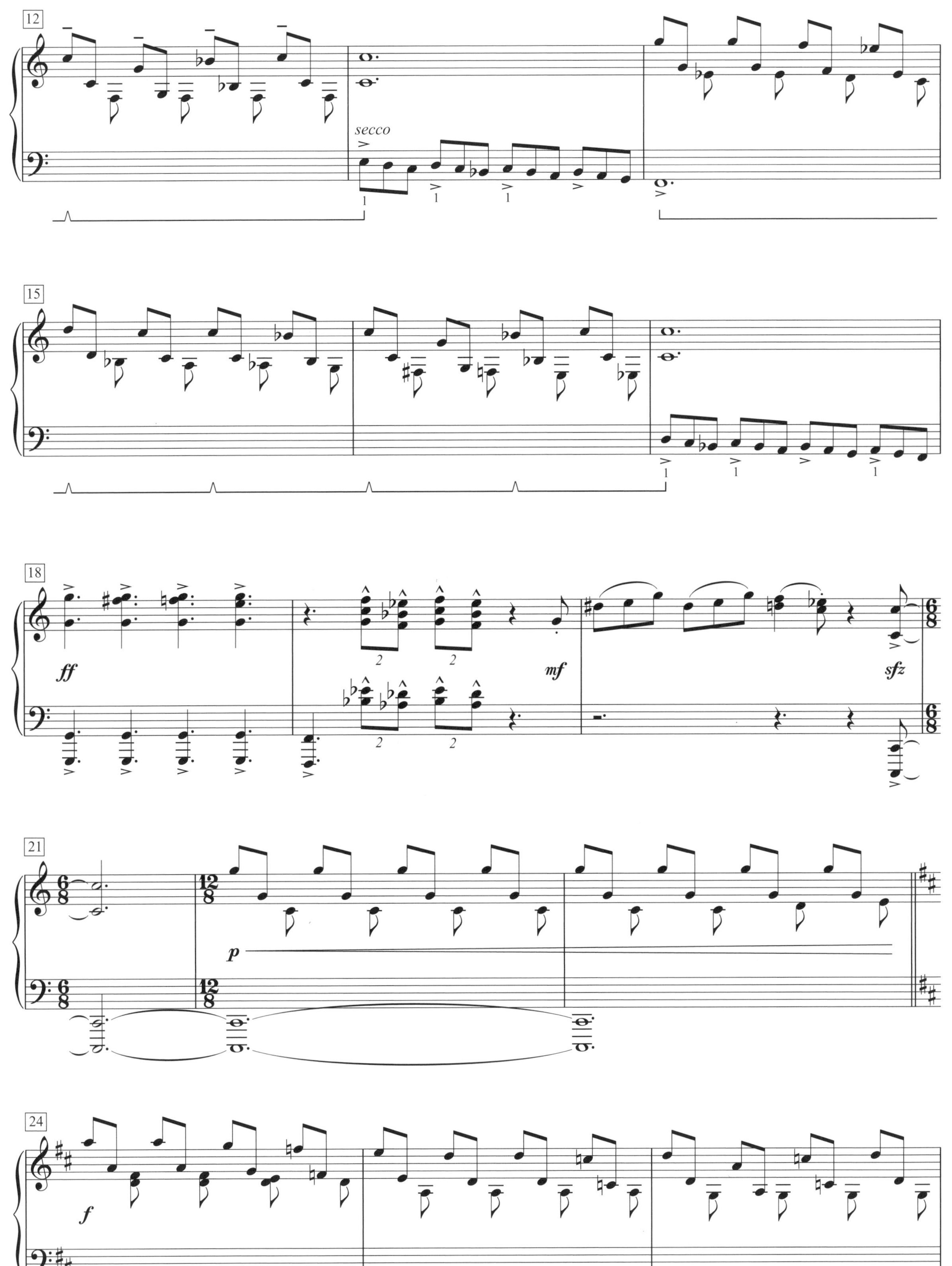

12
secco
15
18
ff
mf
sfz
21
p
24
f

27
secco

30
ff

33
f
rit.

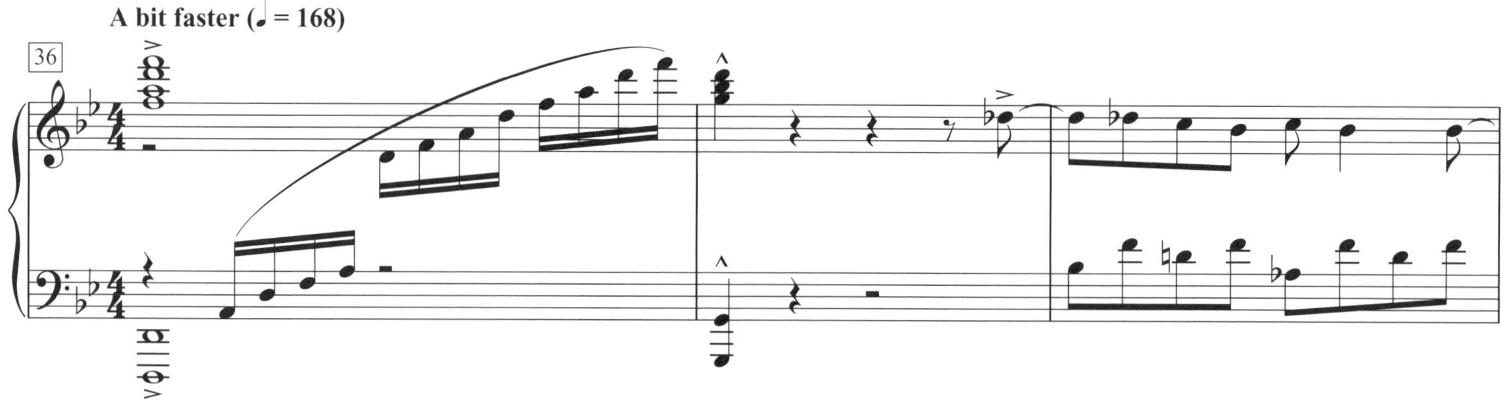
A bit faster (♩ = 168)
36

39

42
(♩. = 144)
mf (L.H.) 1
1-5
(no pedal)
45
sim.
p
48
f
51
54
p
ff
p

57
(♩ = 168)
f
60
ff
6
63
AND I LOVE HER
Passionately (♩ = c. 108)
mp
66
f
69
p

72
rit.
f a tempo
75
p
78
81
f
rit.
p
a tempo
85
rit.
(♩ = 88)
mf

88
4
2 1 2 1
1 2 1 2
90
p
92
f
dim. e rit.
95
p
a tempo
Maestoso (♩ = c. 96)
99
ff
6
6

102
6
6
105
rit.
a tempo
108
mf
111
f
dim. e rit.
115
mp a tempo
molto rit.
pp

I'LL BE BACK
Energetic (♩ = 138)
119
123
127
131
134
f
mp
8vb
R.H.

138
p
141
f
145
mp
148
f
R.H.
150
cantabile

153

broaden

157

rit.

161

a tempo

sfz

165

ff

169

Driving (𝅗𝅥 = 138)

sffz

molto rit.

A HARD DAY'S NIGHT
173
p sub.
177
8va
mf
p
181
8va
f
mp
185
mp
189
f
p

193
f
mp
196
f
199
203
206

Flowing (♩ = c. 116)
209
mf
212
214
rit.
Aggressively (♩ = 126)
217
ff
219

221
223
226
229
232
mf warmly
rit.
f

With grandeur (𝅗𝅥 = c. 100–104)
235
ff
239
243
molto rit.
(𝅗𝅥 = 126)
245
rit.
248
sffz

HELP!

Words and Music by JOHN LENNON
and PAUL McCARTNEY
Arranged by Phillip Keveren

17
p
HELP!
3
21
2
1
4
25
mf
p
29
33
f
p
f

37
sfz p
40
f
44
mp
rit.
f
47
p a tempo
51
R.H. over L.H.
mf

55
R.H. over L.H.
59
f
62
10
6
p
65
f
p
f
69
sfz p
f

73
mp
rit.
f
77
81
dim.
Pulsing steadily (♩ = 132)
p
85
TICKET TO RIDE
mf
89
f

92
8va
mp
4
f
96
2
1
100
103
5
3
3
2
1
106
4
3
3
3

109
mp
f
113
p sub.
117
120
p sub.
123
rit.
Cantabile (♩ = c. 96)
p

126
cresc.
129
f
132
rit. e dim.
p a tempo
135
mp
mf
rit.
f
138
(♩ = 126)
p

141
145
Deeply expressive (♩ = c. 92)
f
mp
148
IT'S ONLY LOVE
f
p
151
153
mf
p
rit.
rit.
a tempo

156
f
rit.
p
f a tempo
159
rit.
p
Soaring (𝅗𝅥 = c. 88)
162
ff
165
168
rit.
(𝅗𝅥 = c. 92)
mf leggiero

171
174
176
rit.
f a tempo
179
rit.
p
(♩ = c. 88)
182
ff

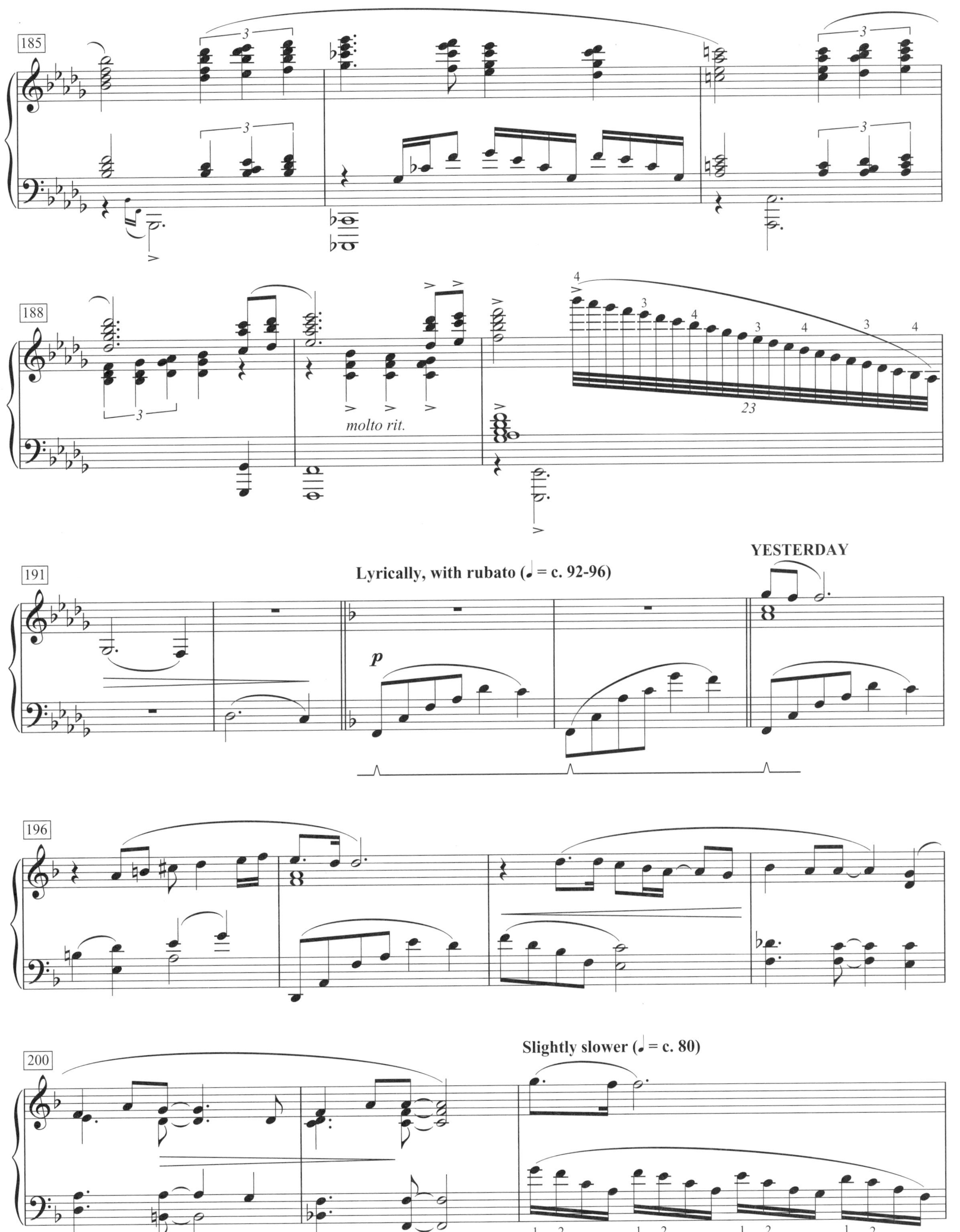
185
3
3
3
3
188
3
molto rit.
4
3
4
3
4
3
4
23
191
Lyrically, with rubato (♩ = c. 92-96)
YESTERDAY
p
196
200
Slightly slower (♩ = c. 80)
1 2
1 2
1 2
1 2

203
mf
12
205
p
208
f
11
210
213
8va
14

(8va)
214
rit.
p
Suddenly very powerful (♩ = c. 84–88)
217
ff
220
11
f
222
molto rit.
225
p
a tempo
pp
rit.
mf
pp

MEET THE BEATLES

Words and Music by JOHN LENNON
and PAUL McCARTNEY
Arranged by Phillip Keveren

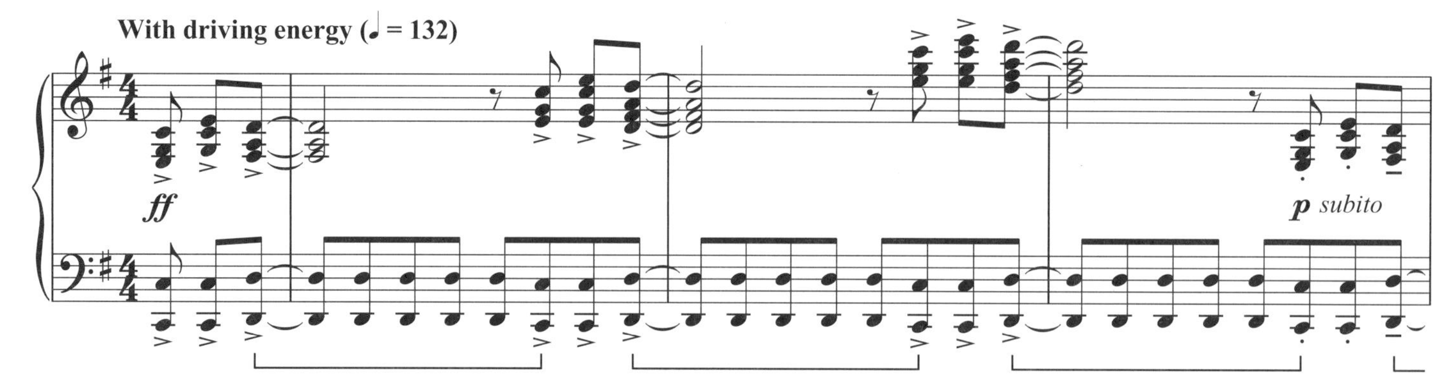

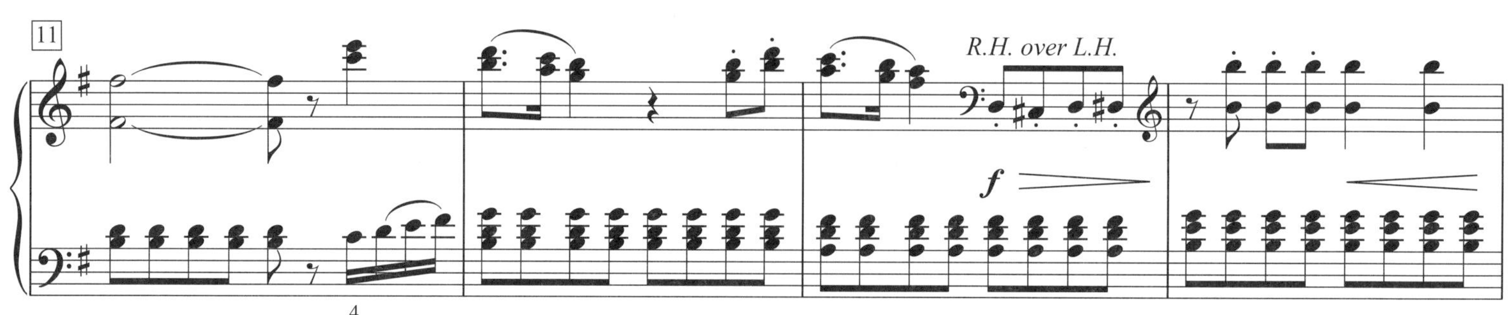

15
8va
19
mf
22
25
28
f

32
35
38
41
mf
44
R.H. over L.H.
f

47
R.H. over L.H.
f

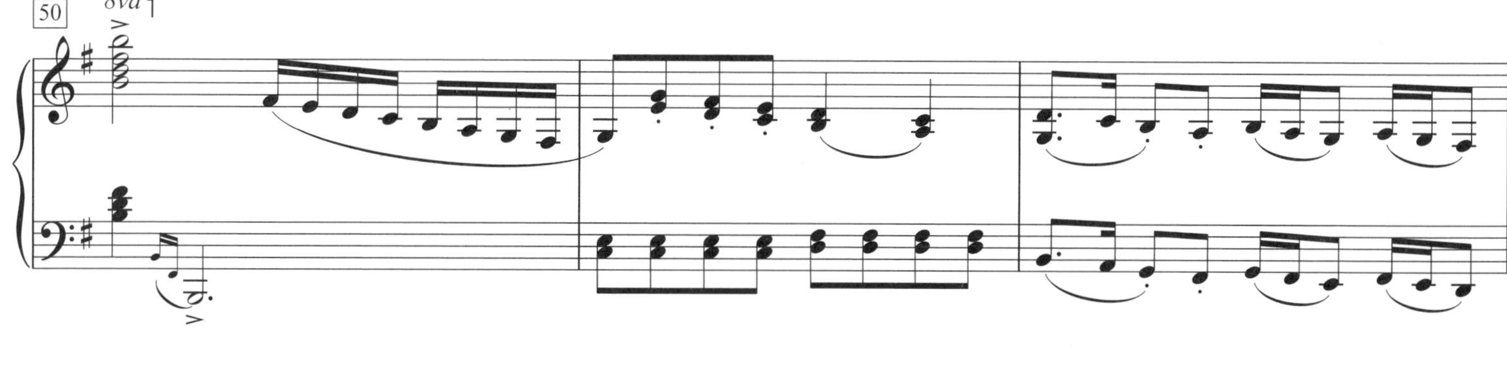
50
8va

53
rit.

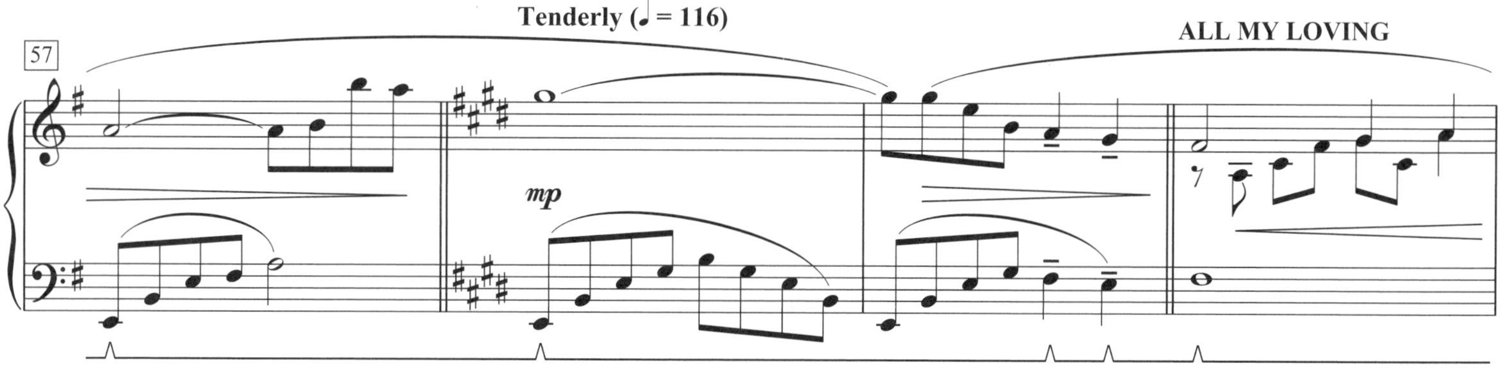
57
Tenderly (♩ = 116)
ALL MY LOVING
mp

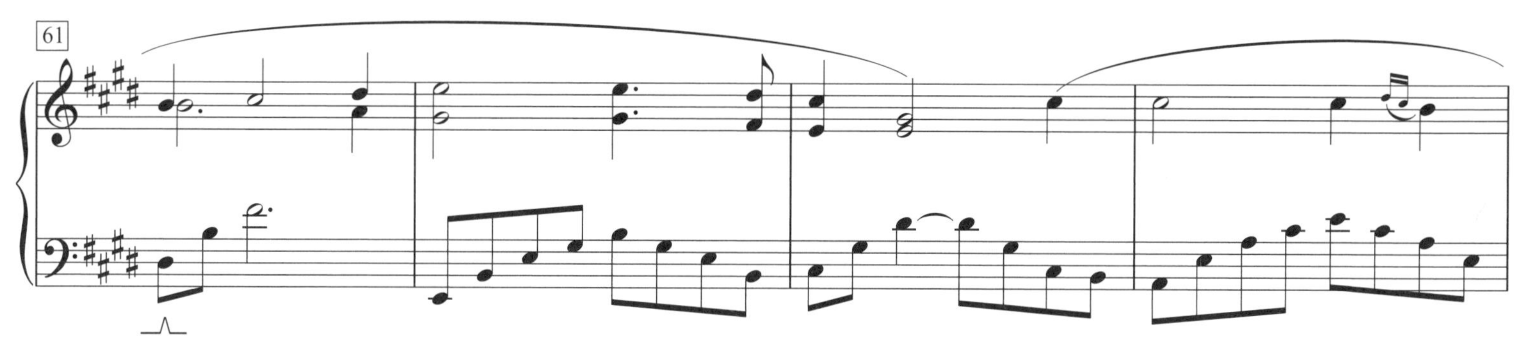
61

65

69
f

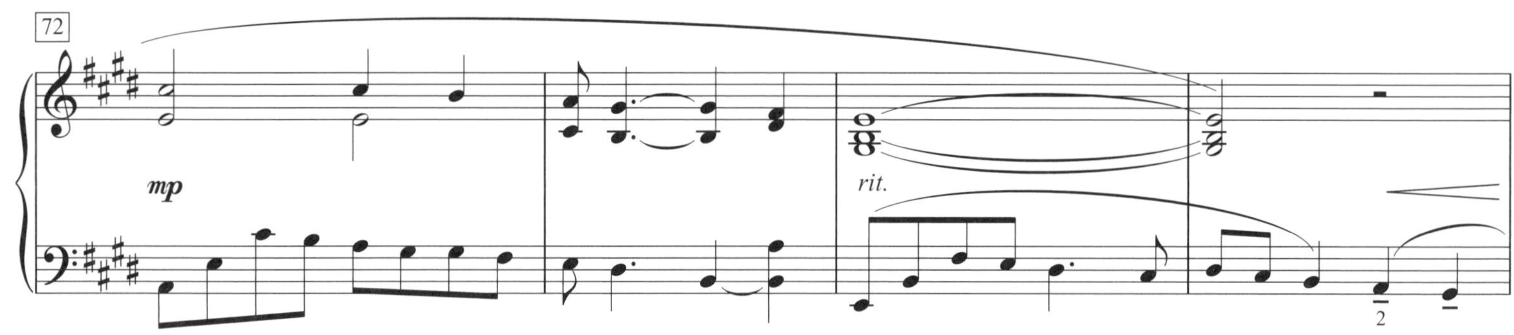
72
mp
rit.

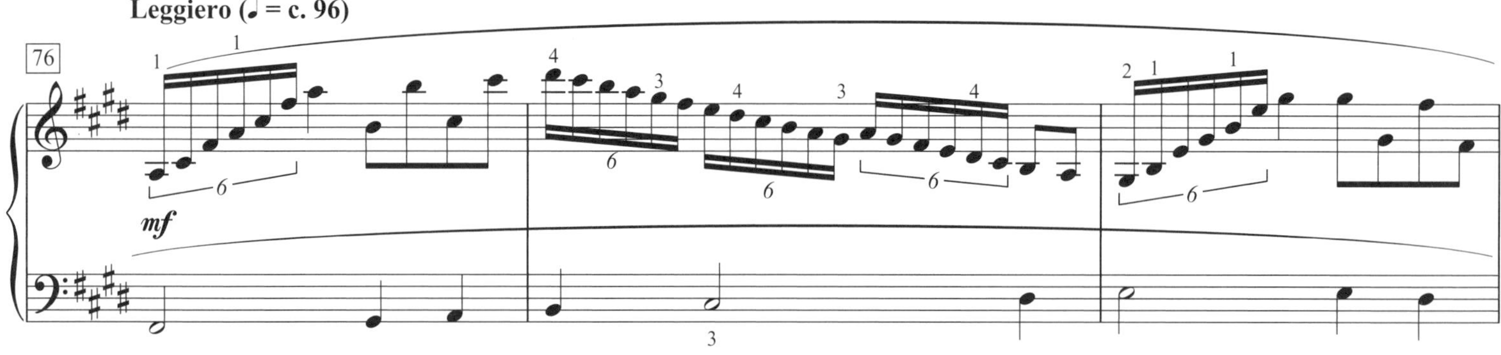
Leggiero (♩ = c. 96)
76
mf

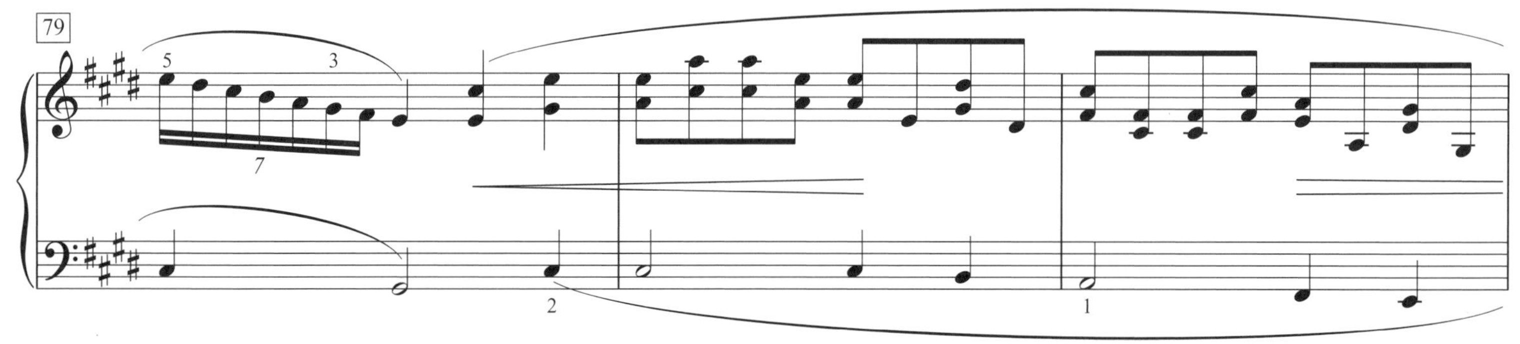
79

82
1
1
1
1
9
p
rit.
f a tempo
85
88
p
rit.
Flowing (♩ = 104)
92
f
94

96
rit.
Precisely (♩. = 126)
98
p
101
mf
104
f
107

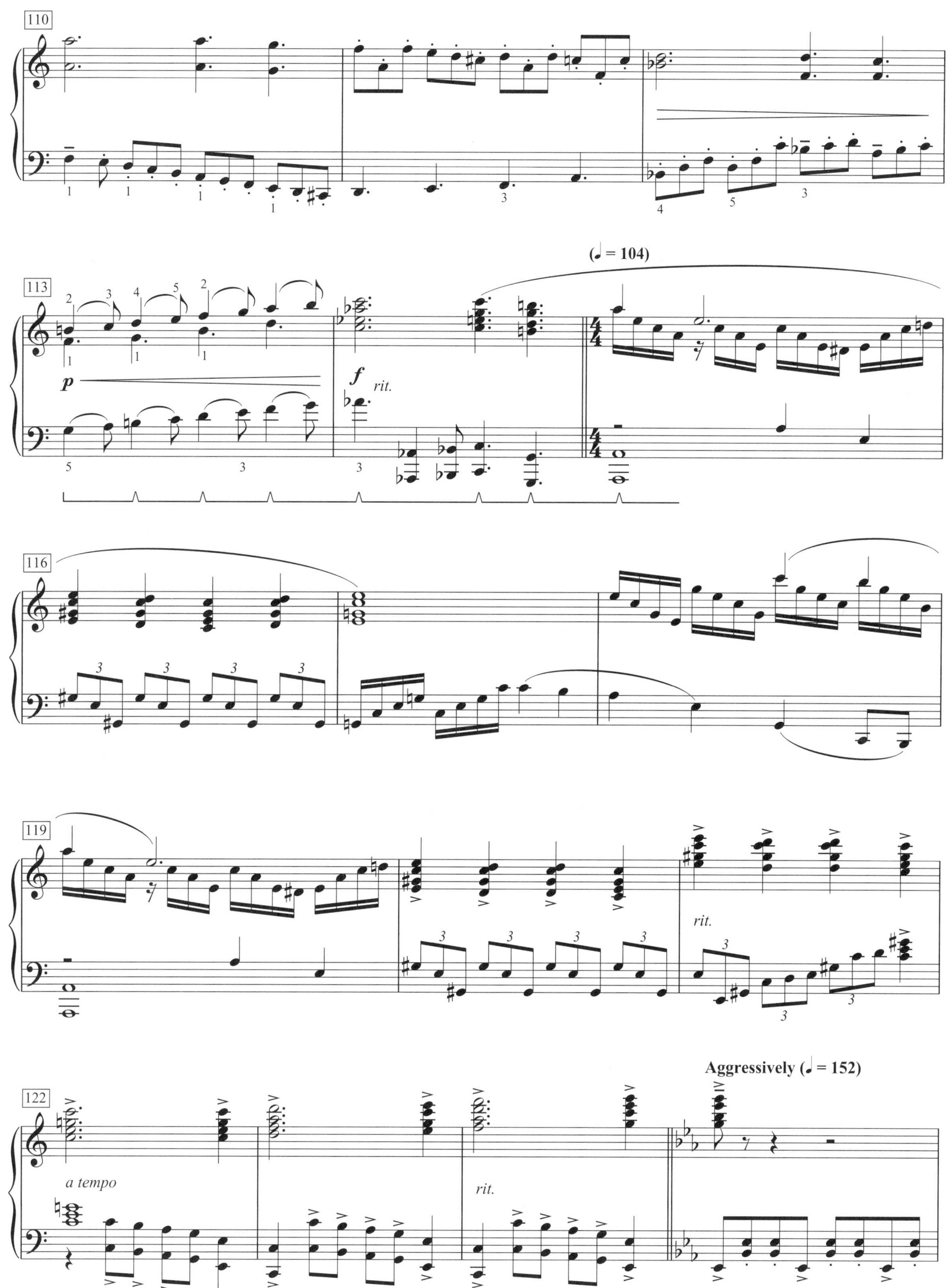
110
113
(♩ = 104)
p
f
rit.
116
119
rit.
122
a tempo
rit.
Aggressively (♩ = 152)

126
IT WON'T BE LONG
130
134
8va
138
142
p cresc.
marcato

146
f
150
154
158
8va
162

165
168
171
175
Slowly, with rubato (♩ = c. 88)
rit.
p
179
mf
molto rit.

I SAW HER STANDING THERE
Vigorously (♩ = 138)
183
p
mf
187
191
f
mf
194
f
197
sfz

201
2

204

207
mf

210

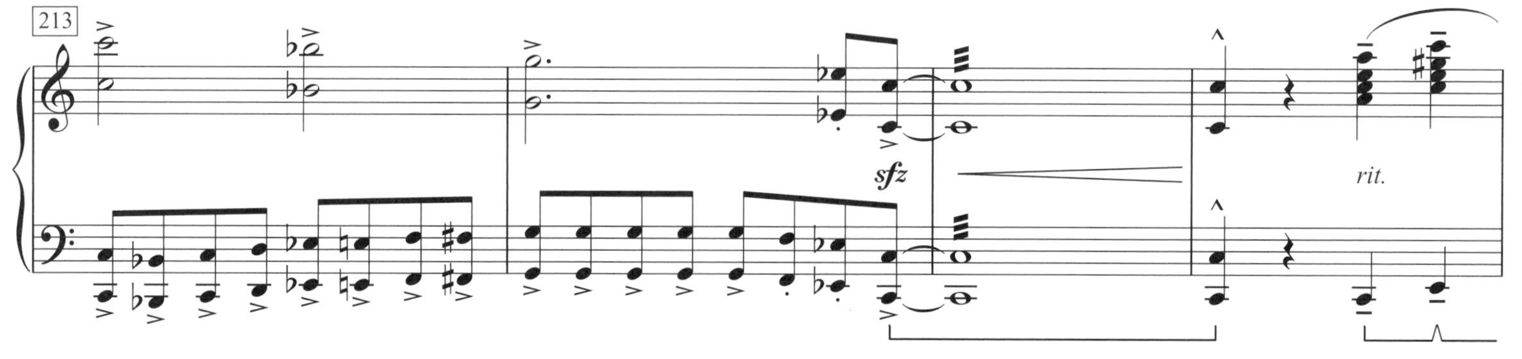
213
sfz
rit.

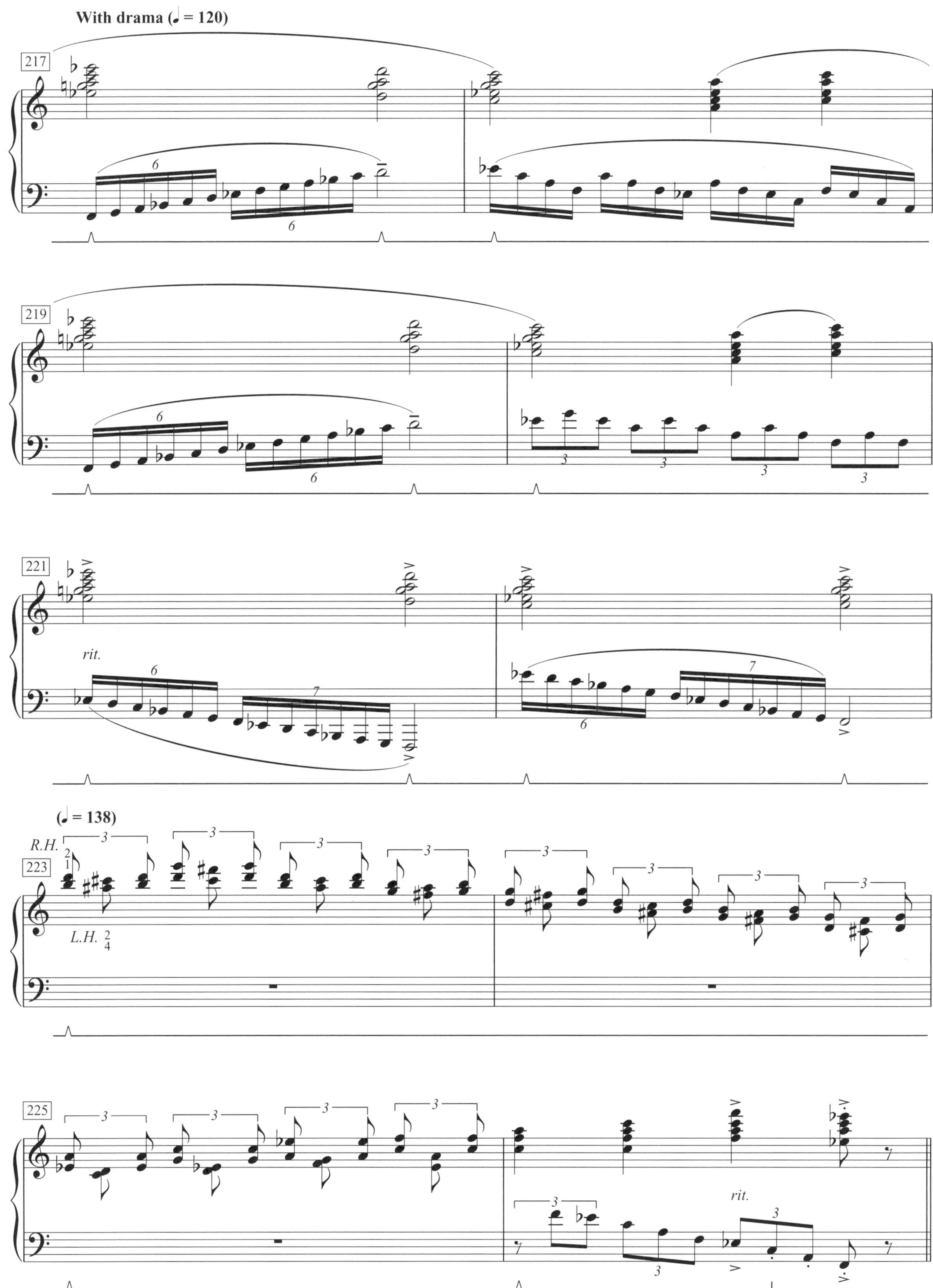
With drama (𝅗𝅥 = 120)
217
6
6
219
6
6
3
3
3
3
221
rit.
6
7
7
6
(𝅗𝅥 = 138)
R.H.
223
L.H.
225
rit.

With abandon
227
a tempo
230
233
mf
236
f
239
sfz
I WANT TO HOLD YOUR HAND (Reprise)
ff

242
sffz
Freely, cadenza-like (♩ = c. 104)
246
mf
f
249
ff
rit.
Presto (♩ = 132)
252
marcato
254

RUBBER SOUL

Words and Music by JOHN LENNON
and PAUL McCARTNEY
Arranged by Phillip Keveren

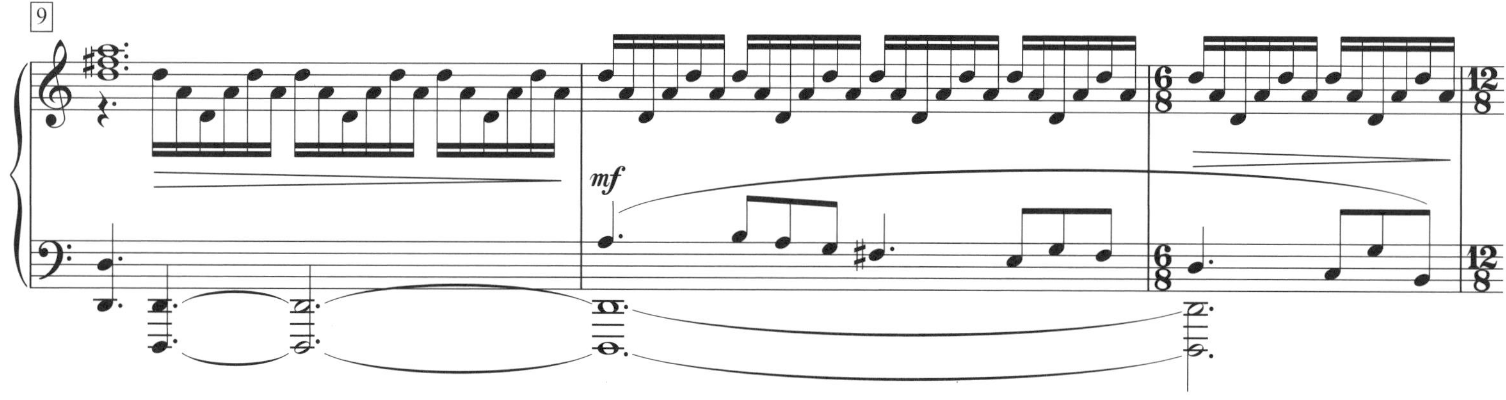

14
18
22
26
29
p

32
f
35
38
41
45
mp

48
f
51
p cresc.
rit.
f
a tempo
54
58
Flowing gently (♩ = c. 100)
62
p
f
p
mp

66
IN MY LIFE
70
p
mf
74
p
mf
78
rit.
pp
82
mf with a Baroque flair
a tempo

85
88
f
91
With grandeur (♩ = 88)
rit.
ff
94
mf
rit.
97
ff a tempo

100
103
106
rit. e dim.
mf
p
MICHELLE
With motion (♩ = 104)
110
mf
p
mf
113

115
p
rit.
f
p
a tempo
118
mf
120
3
f
123
125
17

127
129
rit.
p
132
Delicately (♩. = 76)
mf
134
136
p rit.

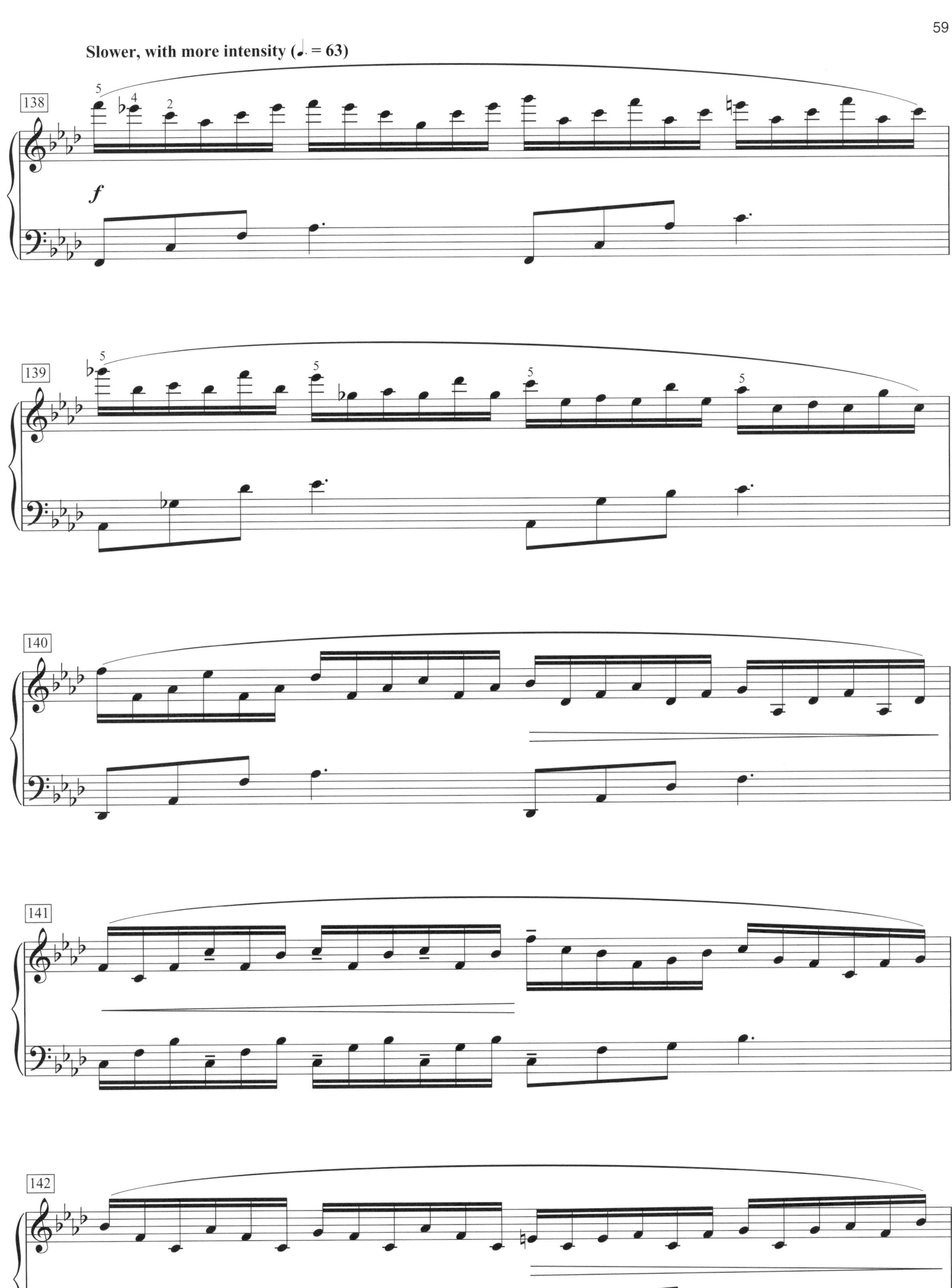
Slower, with more intensity (♩. = 63)
138
139
140
141
142

143

p

144

f rit.

p

146 (♩ = 84)

f

149

rit.

p

151 Soaring (♩. = 69)

ff

153
NORWEGIAN WOOD (This Bird Has Flown)
mf
155
157
p
159
f
161
mf

163
f
rit. e dim.
165
p
a tempo
167
169
mf
171

172
f
rit.
174
With strength (♩. = 50)
ff
rit.
176
(♩. = 69)
178
179
p

181
182
f
rit.
Maestoso (♩ = 160)
184
ff
188
rit.
191
8va
8vb